Sing with the Choir

FOR DUMMIES®

**Performance Notes by
Adam Perlmutter**

ISBN: 978-1-4234-7390-9

HAL•LEONARD®
CORPORATION
7777 W. BLUEMOUND RD. P.O. BOX 13819 MILWAUKEE, WI 53213

Visit Hal Leonard Online at
www.halleonard.com

Table of Contents

Introduction

Welcome to *Sing with the Choir For Dummies*. Here you'll find all the ingredients needed for singing some of the world's most popular songs in a variety of genres, everything from Louis Armstrong's "What a Wonderful World" to Elvis Presley's "Can't Help Falling in Love" to Stevie Wonder's "You Are the Sunshine of My Life." This exciting music includes complete choral arrangements for soprano, alto, tenor, and bass, piano accompaniment parts, and a professionally recorded choir on CD. Enjoy!

About This Book

For each song, I include a bit of background information to satisfy the historically curious. The information is followed by a variety of tidbits that struck me as I made my way through the teaching of these songs, including some of the following:

✔ A run-down of the parts you need to know.

✔ A breakdown of some of the chord progressions important to playing the song effectively.

✔ Some of the critical information you need to navigate the sheet music.

✔ Some tips and shortcuts you can use to expedite the learning process.

In many cases, you may already know how to do a lot of this. If so, feel free to skip over those familiar bits.

How to Use This Book

The music in this book contains choral and piano parts for each song. The song notes included contain handy performance tips that help you learn how to sing these songs and understand how they work. I recommend that you first sing through the song, and then practice all the main sections. From there, you can add the many tricks and treats of each one. Approach each song one section at a time and then assemble the sections together in a sequence. This technique helps to provide you with a greater understanding of how the song is structured, and enables you to learn it more quickly.

In order to follow the music and our performance notes you need a basic understanding of scales and chords. But if you're not a wiz, don't worry. Just spend a little time with the nifty tome *Music Theory For Dummies* by Michael Pilhofer and Holly Day (Wiley), and with a little practice, you'll be on your way to entertaining family and friends.

Conventions Used in This Book

As you might expect, I use quite a few musical terms in this book. Some of these may be unfamiliar to you, so here are a few right off the bat that can help your understanding of basic music principles:

✔ **Bridge:** Part of the song that is different from the verse and the chorus, providing variety and connecting the other parts of the song to each other.

✔ **Chorus:** The part of the song that is the same each time through, usually the most familiar section.

✔ **Coda:** The section at the end of a song, which is sometimes labeled with the word *coda.*

✔ **Hook:** A familiar, accessible, or sing-along melody, lick, or other section of the song.

✔ **Unison:** Two or more voice parts singing the same pitch.

✔ **Verse:** The part of the song that tells the story; each verse has different lyrics, and each song generally has between two and four of these.

Icons Used in This Book

In the margins of this book are several handy icons to help make following the performance notes easier:

A reason to stop and review advice that can prevent personal injury to your singing voice, your brain, or your ego.

These are optional parts, or alternate approaches that those who'd like to find their way through the song with a distinctive flair can take. Often these are slightly more challenging routes, but encouraged nonetheless, because there's nothing like a good challenge!

This is where you will find notes about specific musical concepts that are relevant but confusing to nonmusical types, stuff that you wouldn't bring up, say, at a frat party or at your kid's soccer game.

You get lots of these tips, because the more suggestions I can offer, the better you'll sing. And isn't that what it's all about?

Any Dream Will Do

from JOSEPH AND THE AMAZING TECHNICOLOR® DREAMCOAT
Music by Andrew Lloyd Webber
Lyrics by Tim Rice
Arranged by Mac Huff

Blue Christmas

Words and Music by Billy Hayes and Jay Johnson
Arranged by Mac Huff

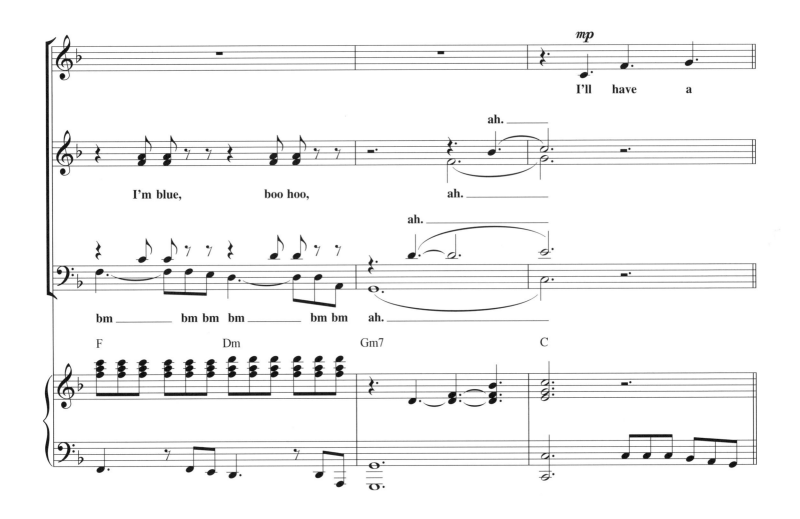

on a green Christ - mas tree

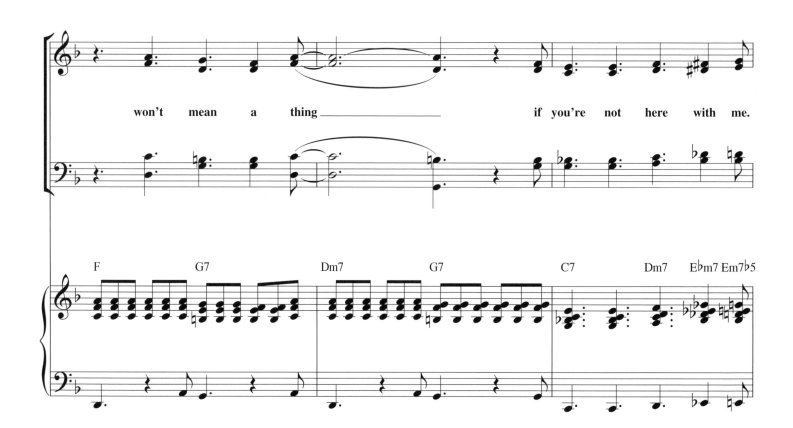

won't mean a thing if you're not here with me.

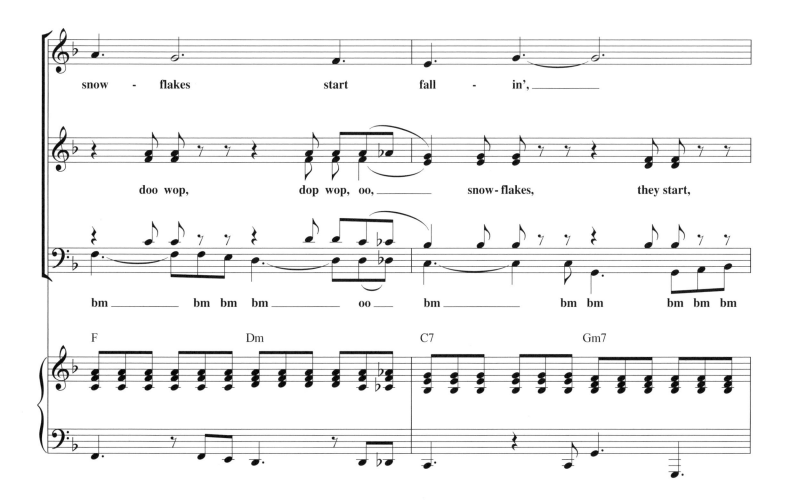

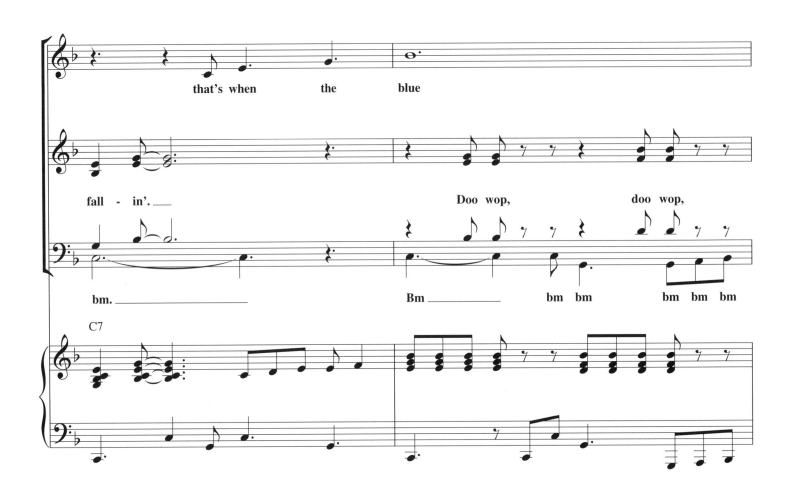

ing.   You'll   be   do   -   in'   all   right ___   with   your

oo.

F   Gm/F   Am7♭5   D7   Am7♭5   D7

But   I'll   have   a

Christ -   mas ___ of ___   white. _____

Gm7   D7   Gm7   Bdim   C7   Gm7

blue,   blue   Christ - mas.

C7sus   C7   F   B♭7

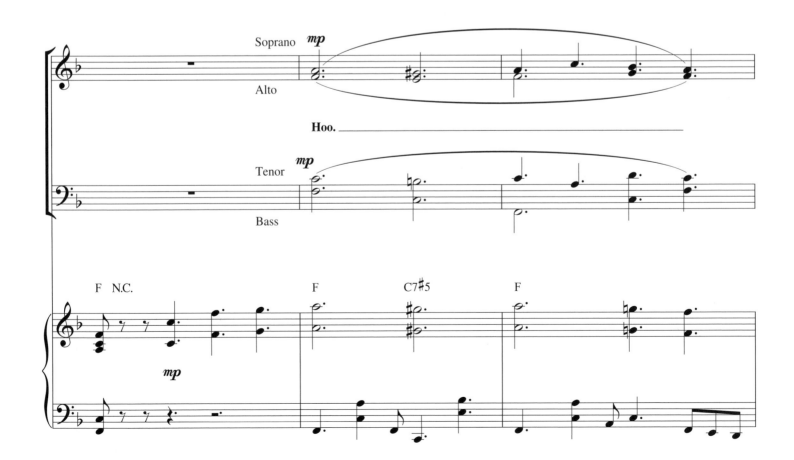

Soprano *mp*

Alto

Hoo.

Tenor *mp*

Bass

F N.C.   F   C7#5   F

mp

I'm blue, so blue, oo, ah.

Bm bm bm bm oo,

I'm feel - in' so blue. Dec - o -

Bm bm bm bm.

ra - tions of red ____ on a green Christ - mas tree ____

_____ won't mean a thing _____ if

hurt - in'. _____

doo wop, hurt - in'. You'll be do - in' all right __

bm _____ bm bm _____ bm oo.

F   C7   F   Gm Am7♭5   D7

___ with your Christ - mas __ of __ white. _____ But

Am7♭5   D7   Gm7   D7 Gm7/D   Bdim

Beauty and the Beast

from Walt Disney's BEAUTY AND THE BEAST
Lyrics by Howard Ashman
Music by Alan Menken
Arranged by Mac Huff

Tale as old as time,   true as it can

Cabaret

from the Musical CABARET
Words by Fred Ebb
Music by John Kander
Arranged by Kirby Shaw

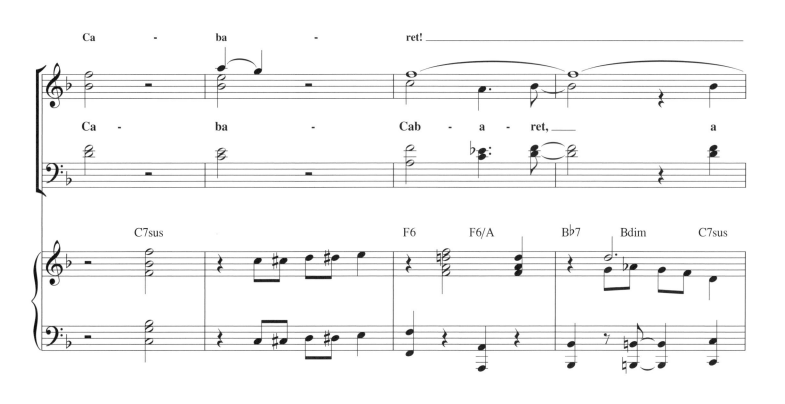

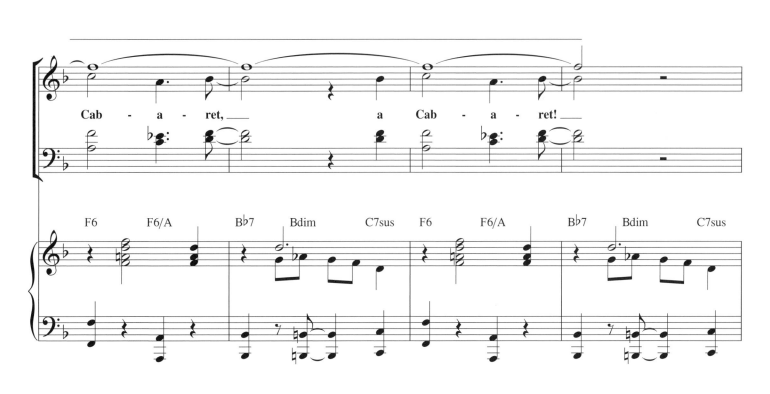

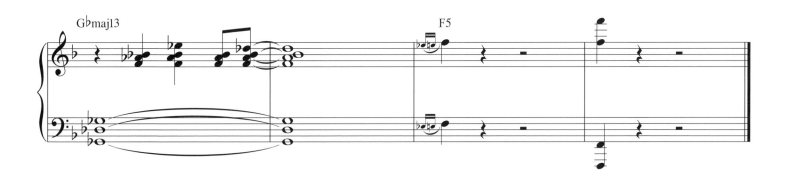

Can't Help Falling in Love

Words and Music by George David Weiss, Hugo Peretti and Luigi Creatore
Arranged by Mark Brymer

TRACK 5

Circle of Life

from Walt Disney Pictures' THE LION KING
Music by Elton John
Lyrics by Tim Rice
Arranged by Keith Christopher

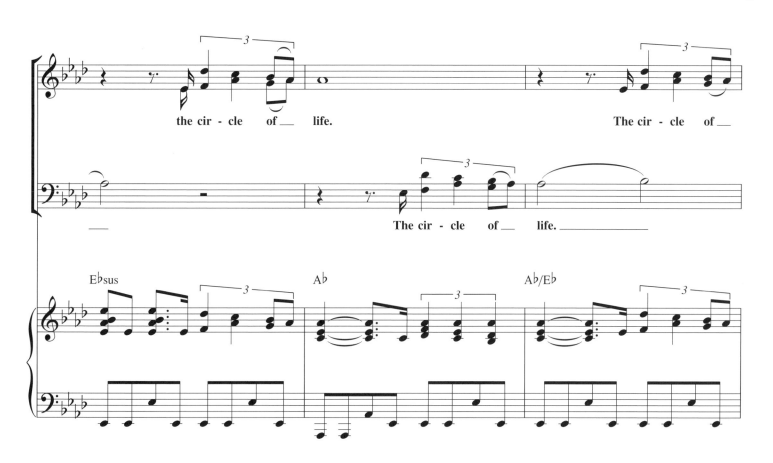

the cir - cle of __ life. The cir - cle of __

The cir - cle of __ life. _____

E♭sus   A♭   A♭/E♭

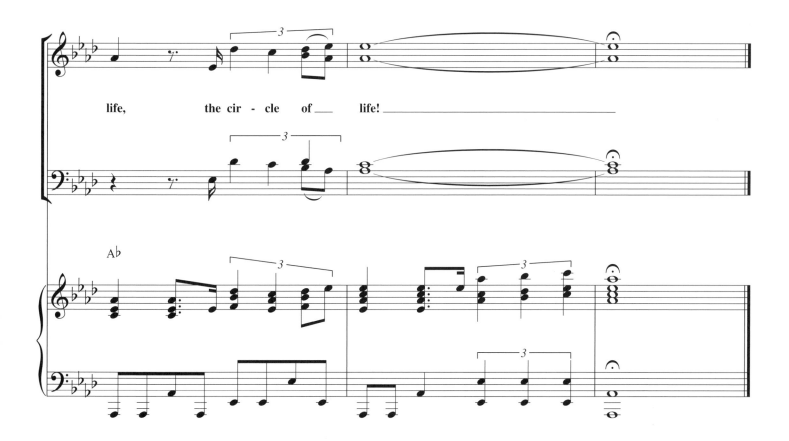

life,   the cir - cle of __ life! _____

A♭

I Dreamed a Dream

from LES MISÉRABLES
Music by Claude-Michel Schönberg
Lyrics by Alain Boublil, Jean-Marc Natel and Herbert Kretzmer
Arranged by Ed Lojeski

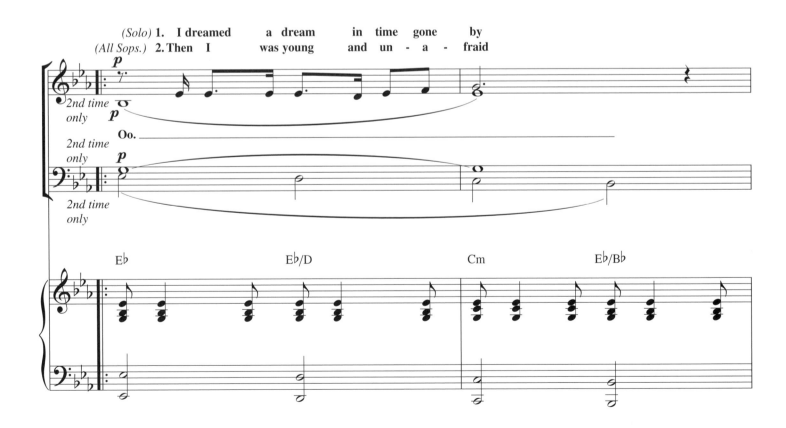

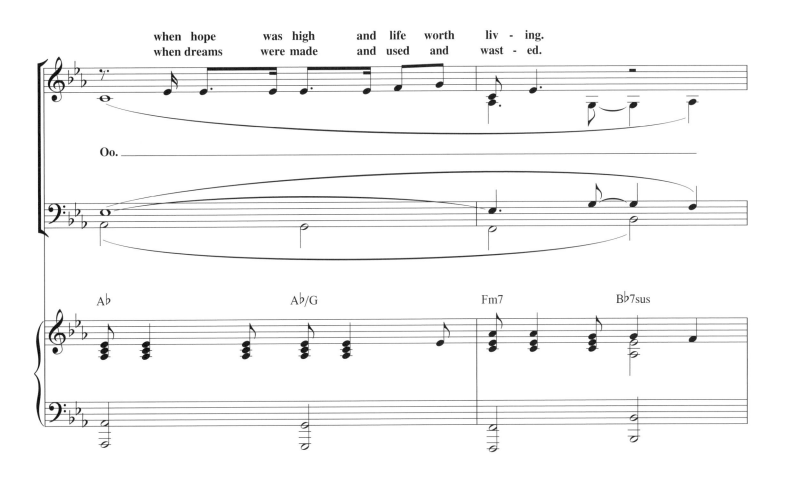

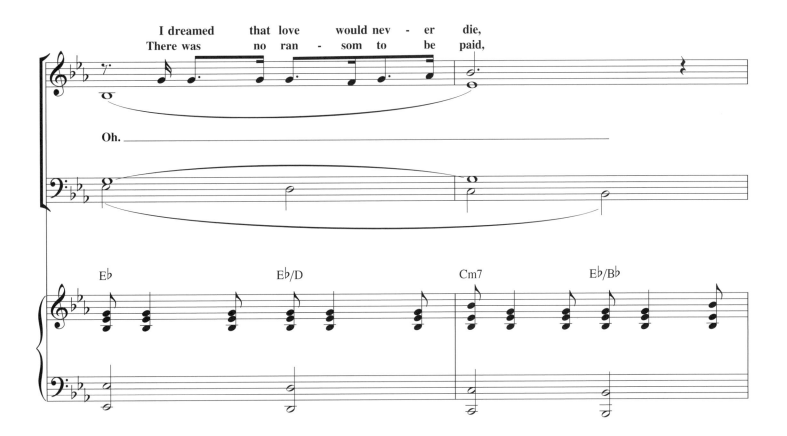

liv - ing, _____ so dif-f'rent now from what it seemed;

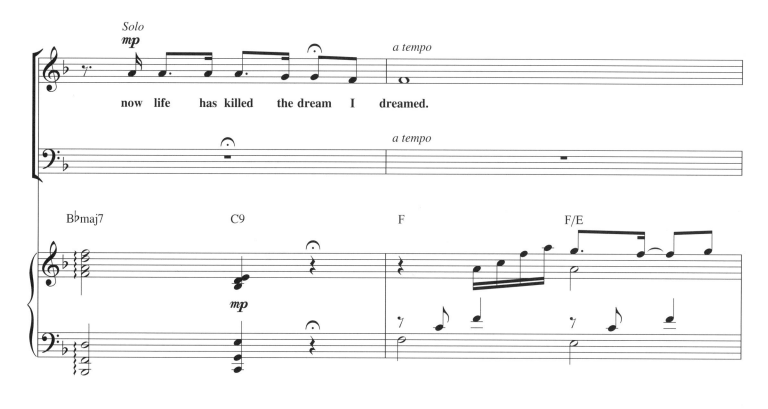

now life has killed the dream I dreamed.

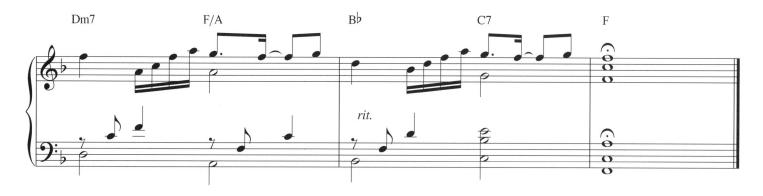

Performance Notes

Any Dream Will Do (page 6/track 1)

For a wildly successful Broadway musical, *Joseph and the Amazing Technicolor Dreamcoat* had a very modest beginning. London's Colet Court Preparatory School originally commissioned it from Andrew Lloyd Webber and Tim Rice. Featuring student performers, the first performance was held on March 1, 1968, and was a mere 15 minutes long. Years later, on January 27, 1982, the show debuted on Broadway and went on to enjoy a run of 749 performances. With its biblical story line and eclectic mix of musical styles from rock to country to disco, *Joseph* remains one of the most popular musicals of all time.

In Act I, the narrator sings "Any Dream Will Do" to a group of children to inspire them to become dreamers. This upbeat tune is arranged here in the key of B♭ major. You'll notice the tempo indicates a lilting swing. This rhythmic feel features prominently in jazz, where a pair of consecutive eighth notes is played not evenly, but long-short, at approximately a ratio of two to one. In the music here, the swing feel is represented by a dotted eighth note followed by a 16th.

Be sure to sing these rhythms with a little bounce — think of the sound of a jazzy hi-hat as you're going through the music. Strong finger snaps where indicated on beats 2 and 4 will also help you feel the rhythm.

Beauty and the Beast (page 32/track 3)

The eighth-longest running production in the history of Broadway, *Beauty and the Beast* saw 5,464 performances between 1994 and 2007. This enchanting musical was based on the 1991 Disney animated film of the same name, in which a prince is transformed into a beast, imprisons a young lady, and must win her love in order to return to his human state. From the movie and the musical, the lovely ballad "Beauty and the Beast" chronicles the love blooming between its eponymous characters.

Scan through our F Major arrangement of "Beauty and the Beast," and you'll see that certain phrases may be sung solo, and that sometimes the separate female (soprano and alto) and male (tenor and bass) voices have separate parts, but other times sing together in unison. Before you sing a note of the song, it would be a good idea to determine if there will be a solo or duet within the piece and to make sure that each singer knows exactly what his or her part is throughout the arrangement.

Blue Christmas (page 17/track 2)

Perhaps no popular song better captures the feeling of being heartbroken during the holidays than "Blue Christmas." The song was originally a country number, recorded in 1948 by Doye O'Dell and popularized by Ernest Tubb the following year. Elvis Presley's famous rock 'n' roll version debuted in 1957, and has since seen many excellent covers by artists as diverse as the '80s rocker Billy Idol, the operatic tenor and multi-instrumentalist Andrea Bocelli, and the indie rock band Bright Eyes.

This arrangement, based in the key of F major, is in a *doo-wop* style — a vocal-based rhythm and blues offshoot that emerged during the 1940s. In a typical doo-wop song, and in this version as well, a small group of background singers support a soloist. The background vocals are usually harmonized and feature nonsense syllables — if you scan the music here you'll see typical utterances like "bm," "doo," and "wop."

This doo-wop arrangement of "Blue Christmas" is written with a 12/8 time signature. If you're unfamiliar with 12/8, just think of it as 12 eighth notes per measure, which you can count "*One,* two, three; *two,* two, three; *three,* two, three; *four,* two, three," and so on, with an emphasis on the first beat of each three-note group.

Focus on your part and take the time to learn it slowly, paying close attention to the rhythmic placement of each note, before joining up with the choir.

Cabaret *(page 40/track 4)*

Cabaret is a musical with a string of antecedents. It's based on the John Van Druten play *I Am a Camera,* which was adapted from the novel *Mr. Norris Changes Trains* and the short-story collection *Goodbye to Berlin,* both by Christopher Isherwood. *Cabaret* debuted on Broadway November 20, 1966 and ran for 1,165 performances. The story takes place in a questionable Berlin nightspot, the Kit Kat Klub, at the time of the Nazis' rise to power. It explores the relationship between a young cabaret performer, Sally Bowles, and an American writer, Cliff Bradshaw; meanwhile, a subplot presents another romance, between a German boardinghouse owner, Fräulein Schneider, and a Jewish fruit seller, Herr Schultz. Belted out by Sally just before the finale, the show's bright title song is its most memorable.

A choral arrangement of "Cabaret" appears here in the key of E♭ major and contains some elements that might bear some explanation. In the first handful of measures you'll see X-shaped note heads positioned at the B above middle C. Disregard this pitch — the Xs simply call for the music to be spoken and not sung. In conjunction with these specialized note heads you'll see a rhythm, the *quarter-note triplet* (three quarter notes in the space normally occupied by two), indicated with the bracketed number three above the notes. To negotiate this rhythm, try counting eighth-note triplets on each beat: "trip-uh-let, trip-uh-let," and so on.

Look out for the pitch *clusters* that occur between the tenor and bass voices. A cluster is comprised of two or more closely spaced notes, and in this case the clusters are a major second apart (B♭ to C). Be sure to listen to your designated note closely where you see a cluster, and fight the temptation to match the pitch of the other notes. Notice that the B♭ and C cluster, along with the corresponding soprano and alto notes, G and E♭, form a Cm7 chord.

Can't Help Falling in Love *(page 52/track 5)*

Though not a household name, George Weiss composed some of pop's most memorable gems from the 1940s though the 1970s. Weiss' songbook includes "What a Wonderful World" and "Can't Help Falling in Love," popularized by Louis Armstrong and Elvis Presley, respectively. Based on the French chanson "Plaisir D'Amour," "Can't Help Falling in Love" was Elvis's signature love song. It was featured in his 1961 film, *Blue Hawaii.* Testament to the song's durability is a 1993 cover by the reggae group UB40 and a 2002 version by the Swedish pop group A-Teens.

"Can't Help Falling in Love" is arranged here in the key of E♭ major. It's critically important to sing this song as expressively as possible, and the dynamic markings shown throughout will help you do so. Take special note of the markings *crescendo* and *decrescendo* that appear throughout. Where you see a hairpin line with a closed beginning (*crescendo*), gradually sing more loudly until the opening of the hairpin sign. Where you see a hairpin line with an open beginning (*decrescendo*), sing gradually more quietly until you reach the point at which the lines close. Soloists and ensemble members alike need to be aware and in control of dynamic changes like these to contribute to a musical performance.

Circle of Life *(page 58/track 6)*

Just like "Beauty and the Beast," "Circle of Life" is from a Disney movie made into a musical. The theatrical incarnation of *The Lion King* debuted on Broadway in October of 1997 and 15 years later it's still running, making it the seventh-longest show in Broadway history. *The Lion King* chronicles the story of a young lion prince, Simba, and the drama that unfolds surrounding his ascendancy to the throne as king. With music by Elton John and lyrics by Tim Rice, "Circle of Life" was a pop hit for John, with his recording of the song hitting #18 on the U.S. charts. Not too shabby for what was ostensibly music for children.

The key to creating a good choir performance of "Circle of Life" is paying attention to the details. In bars 2 and 5, for instance, tenors and basses should not ignore the articulation markings. The curved line preceding each C calls for a *scoop*. Vocally glide into that note from a nonspecific pitch below. Meanwhile the dot above each note in these measures is a *staccato*, which calls for the note to be sung a bit shorter than its designated note value. Also be sure to observe the *crescendo* and *decrescendo* markings, which add a bit of emotional heft to the proceedings (see the notes for "Can't Help Falling in Love" for more on the topic).

I Dreamed a Dream *(page 70/track 7)*

Les Misérables, a masterpiece about the beginnings of the French revolution by the 19th century novelist Victor Hugo, was the source for the great musical of the same name. *Les Mis,* as it is commonly called, opened in Paris on September 17, 1980, in London's West End five years later, and then on Broadway in 1987. The show is still being staged in both London and New York, making it the longest-running musical ever. With music by composer Claude-Michel Schönberg, *Les Misérables* features a number of memorable tunes, most notably "I Dreamed a Dream," which has become a pop standard of sorts, having been covered by everyone from Neil Diamond to Aretha Franklin.

One of the things that make this arrangement interesting is the number of different textures it contains. In the first couple of bars, check out how the soprano takes the lead while the tenors accompany with long whole notes on the syllable "Oo," and the basses sing a descending line in half notes on the same syllable. In contrast, the sopranos and altos sing a unison phrase in bar 12, then they rest while the tenors and basses reply in the following measure. Because of these textural changes, the music is as fun to listen to as it is to sing. Be sure to familiarize yourself with your part in its entirety before you begin. Tenors and baritones, note the *divisi* in bar 21. The music is divided here: the higher tenors sing a D and the lower tenors sing a B♭, while the higher basses sing an F and the lower basses another B♭, combining to form a resounding B♭ major chord.

I Left My Heart in San Francisco *(page 84/track 8)*

San Francisco, that city by the Bay, has inspired a number of great songs, including this one, popularized in 1962 by the pop singer Tony Bennett. It was written in 1954 by Douglass Cross and George Cory, a pair who had recently moved to New York City, clearly deeply nostalgic for their gentler West Coast hometown. This beautiful tune has been covered by vocal greats like Frank Sinatra and even the R&B singer Bobby Womack. Meanwhile, five decades after Bennett first recorded the song, it remains a staple of his live set.

Based in the key of B♭ major, the first eleven bars contain separate solos for male and female voices. Conveniently, the range of notes in the former can be covered by either a soprano or an alto; the latter, by either a tenor or bass, so select your choir's star male and female singers for the solos. Note that the music is to be sung *rubato,* that is to say, with disregard for a strict tempo. Sing the music very freely here, adhering to the prescribed rhythms but speeding up or slowing down at your own discretion. Remember that this is a song about heartsickness, so whether you're taking the lead or blending in with the choir, sing "I Left My Heart in San Francisco" with as much feeling as you can muster.

A couple of other details to look out for: Be sure to closely follow the dynamic markings throughout, for maximum expressiveness. Four bars from the end, where you see the marking *rit. e cresc. (ritardando and crescendo),* simply sing slower and louder. In the next measure and in the terminal one, too, the semicircle with the dot inside is a *fermata* sign — hold the note longer than the designated value. One last thing, in the penultimate bar, heads-up on the sneaky time signature change, to 6/4 (six quarter notes per bar) from 4/4.

Kansas City *(page 92/track 9)*

Kansas City and its own brand of hard-swinging jazz were the inspiration for the Jerry Leiber and Mike Stoller song named after this great Midwestern town. The song was first recorded in 1952 by the R&B singer Little Willie Littlefield, and seven years later it became a hit for another R&B singer, Wilbert Harrison, and the rocker Little Richard. With its swinging beat, "Kansas City" is undeniably great fun to sing with the choir.

Key to making "Kansas City" come alive is to really nail the rhythms. The first order of business is to acknowledge the swing feel. In this arrangement, when you see a pair of eighth notes, don't sing them evenly — sing the first one longer than the second. If you find yourself having trouble with this rhythmic feel, spend a little time listening to the recording. Then, with the sheet music at hand, try singing the rhythms in this swing style.

Another thing to listen for are the blue notes — the flatted thirds (D♭, or E♭ when the piece modulates to C major) that occur throughout this song. Heard commonly in blues, jazz, and rock, a *blue note* is a simple alteration that gives the music a very soulful quality. A true blue note actually falls somewhere between a major and a minor third, and everyone in your choir will get bonus points if they can articulate this microtonal inflection.

Let It Be *(page 112/track 11)*

Many listeners think that the Beatles' "Let It Be," with the lyric "Mother Mary," is religious in nature. However, the Mary in this song is Paul McCartney's mother, who died when he was only 14 years old. As an adult, Paul had a dream that he was rejoined with his mother and she told him, "It will be all right, just let it be." This lyrical idea received a piano theme, and one of the greatest songs in the Beatles' catalog, in fact in all of rock 'n' roll history, was born.

In this arrangement, "Let It Be" is transposed to the key of F major from the original key of C major. In terms of pitch content, this song is easy to sing, because accidentals are used very sparingly. The rhythms, on the other hand, with their extensive 16th-note syncopation, might prove tricky for some. And something to consider, of course, is that a shaky sense of rhythm can affect your sense of pitch. If you experience any difficulty in learning your part, just take things very slowly and *subdivide.* Count, "One-ee-and-uh, two-ee-and-uh, three-ee-and-uh, four-ee-and-uh," and so on. The good news is that once you've internalized this rhythm, the rest of the song will be easier to learn, as will 16th-note syncopations you encounter in other pieces of music.

Love Me Tender *(page 124/track 12)*

One of Elvis Presley's best-known numbers, "Love Me Tender" was the theme song to not just one, but *31* of the King's motion pictures. When listeners first heard the song in 1956, it probably sounded familiar to some. That's because the melody was adapted from "Aura Lee," a Civil War ballad. Throughout the years, "Love Me Tender" has been covered by a range of artists, including the bluesman B.B. King, the country crooner Merle Haggard, and the funk master James Brown. And as you'll see, the song lends itself nicely to a choral arrangement.

Although "Love Me Tender," arranged here in the key of G major, is melodically straightforward, it's got some *chromatic* (falling outside of the key) pitches here and there that could be potentially problematic. In bar 13, for instance, the tenor voice contains a C♯, known as a *chromatic lower neighbor* to the Ds in the surrounding measures. Similarly, in bar 15 the alto contains an E♭ functioning as a *chromatic passing tone,* connecting two notes within the key of G: E♮ and D. Having faulty intonation on pitches like these can wreck an otherwise decent choral performance, so for the good of the group, if you have any uncertainty when you practice your part, use a piano until you can hear and sing the chromatic notes with confidence.

Moon River *(page 103/track 10)*

"Moon River," with lyrics by Johnny Mercer and music by Henry Mancini, was inspired by Mercer's formative experiences as a Southern lad, and was first heard in the 1961 motion picture *Breakfast at Tiffany's,* sung by Audrey Hepburn. The popular singer and television host Andy Williams liked the song so much that he sang the first eight bars as an introduction to his show, and many artists have likewise made it their own — from the jazz legend Louis Armstrong to the soul singer Aretha Franklin to the rock group R.E.M. You can do the same with this beautiful choral arrangement.

"Moon River" kicks off here in the key of B♭ major. Though the music shouldn't be too difficult to sing, it would be a good idea to scan through the sheet music first, to make sure you understand the overall structure and all the smaller details. Be sure to take note of all the expressive and tempo markings. For instance, on the last system of the first page the indication *accel.* calls for you to speed up; *rit.,* to slow down; and *a tempo,* to return to the original tempo. You might want to take a pencil and mark any spots that could use a little extra attention, like the parts where separate voices join in unison; the time signature change to 3/4 at the end of the first page; and the modulation, up a major second to the key of C major, at the end of the following page. Incidentally, when you sing the tune, enjoy how the key change adds a little emotional lift.

Silver Bells *(page 132/track 13)*

Salvation Army workers ringing bells for charity on sidewalks during the holiday season were the inspiration for "Silver Bells," a Christmas song with a bustling urban setting rather than the traditional peaceful rural backdrop. The song was first heard in the 1951 motion picture *The Lemon Drop Kid,* starring Bob Hope and Marilyn Maxwell. In its illustrious recorded history the song has been interpreted by everyone from the gospel great Mahalia Jackson to the folk/rock legend Bob Dylan to the singing cowboy Gene Autry. Here, it receives a festive choral treatment.

Many singers are familiar with "Silver Bells," arranged here in the key of G major. The melody is pretty simple and the rhythms square. Because of that, it's important to take care when singing this song and zero in on any potentially troublesome spot. Each singer should be mindful of the leaps, like the *perfect fifth* in bar 5 and the *octave* in bar 11, in the solo section that begins this arrangement. In instances like these it can be easy to overshoot the interval and sing sharp. Heads up on the descending chromatic line sung by the altos! This begins in bar 13. Be sure to take a full breath before singing this phrase, to avoid singing flat.

What a Wonderful World (page 142/track 14)

Some purists regard the music that jazz pioneer Louis Armstrong created late in his career as inauthentic. But there is no denying that Armstrong's signature number during this period, "What a Wonderful World," is a genuinely good song — a tune so sweet that even a veteran punk-rocker like Joey Ramone couldn't resist it, evidenced in his posthumously released 2002 cover. The spirit of this arrangement, though, is closer to Armstrong's original 1968 recording, in other words, slightly more polite.

"What a Wonderful World" begins here in the key of F major and smoothly modulates up a half step, to G♭ at bar 27. A variety of different writing approaches make this arrangement pleasurable to sing. In the first few bars, for example, the sopranos and altos sing in harmonized sixths, a particularly sweet-sounding interval, while the basses sit out. Then, in bar 7 when the lower voices enter, they join to form a full D♭ major triad. Next, the sopranos and altos sing in unison as do the tenors and basses, with the two groups singing an octave apart. Textural variations like these keep music exciting and interesting to the listener, so bear this in mind should you ever find yourself writing choral arrangements.

You Are the Sunshine of My Life (page 150/track 15)

In the early 1970s, the R&B singer-songwriter Stevie Wonder, toying around on his electric piano, happened upon an inspiring riff. This instrumental evolved into the bright song, "You Are the Sunshine of My Life," released in 1973 on the album *Talking Book*. Instantly popular, with great crossover appeal, it appeared simultaneously on the pop, R&B, and adult contemporary charts. This arrangement turns the solo vocal number into a soulful choral excursion.

The music starts here in the key of F major and modulates up a step, to G major, midway through the tune. The melody should be fairly easy for all voices to sing because it contains mostly stepwise motion, and this arrangement avoids some of the *melismatic* (many notes falling on a single syllable) flourishes that are Wonder's trademark. But the arrangement does preserve the extensive syncopation found in the original, and in order for this to work as a choral piece, all voices have to be locked in tightly on the rhythm. If you're at all insecure about the syncopations, it would be a good idea to spend time learning your part slowly and subdividing, feeling the pulse in eighth notes rather than quarters, counting, "One-and, two-and, three-and, four-and," and so on. Listening and singing along with the CD is another good way to practice. Remember, no matter how beautiful your singing voice is, you won't have a very large audience if you don't have a good sense of rhythm.

I Left My Heart in San Francisco

Words by Douglass Cross
Music by George Cory
Arranged by Ed Lojeski

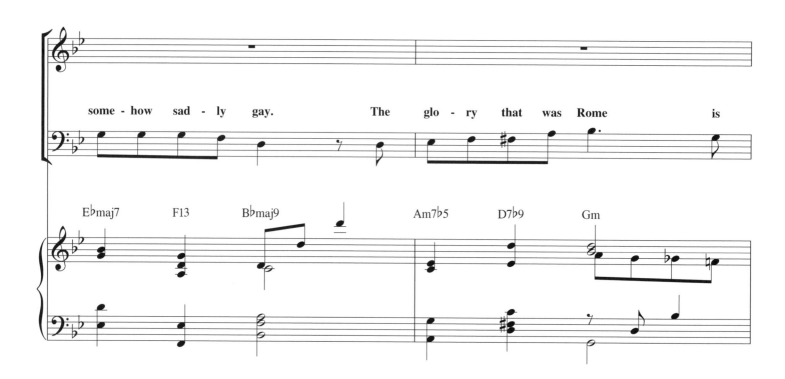

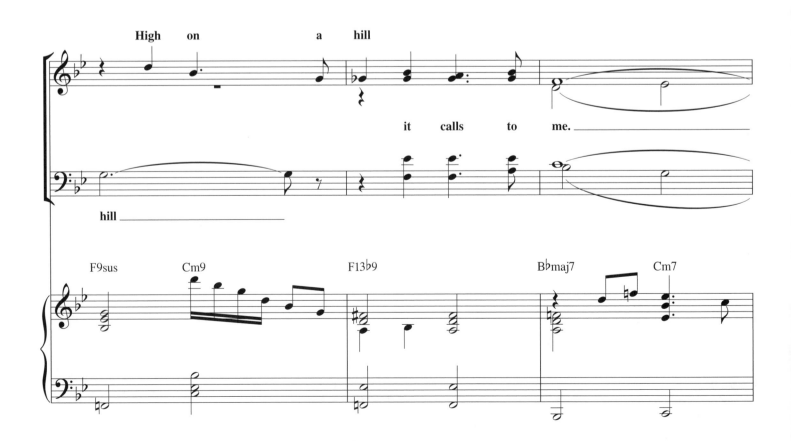

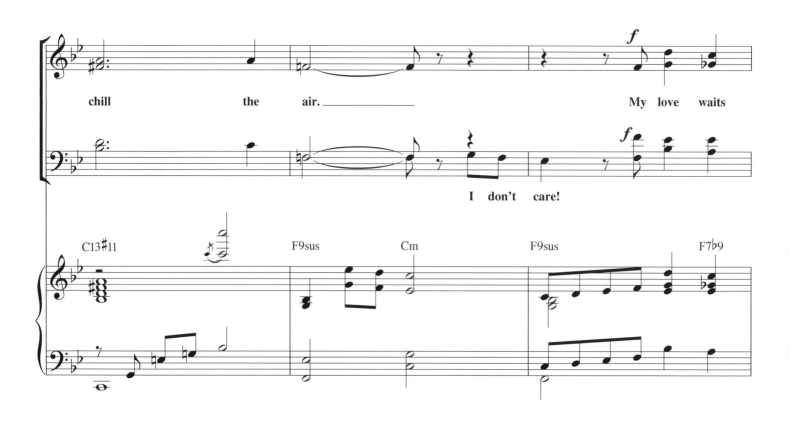

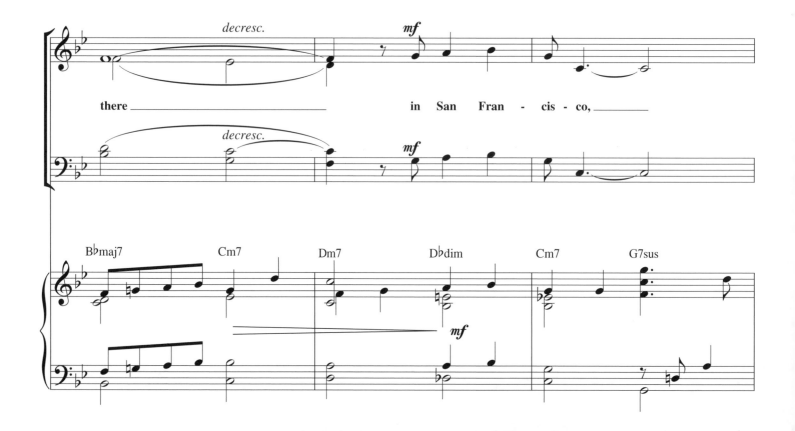

your gold - en sun   will shine for me.

C9   B9   C9   F9sus   G+/F   F13sus   F13♭9   B♭maj13   Am

When   I   come   home   to   you,

When   I   come   When   I   come   home   San Fran -

home   to   you,   San Fran -

When   I   come   home

G13   Cm7   G13   F/A   G/B

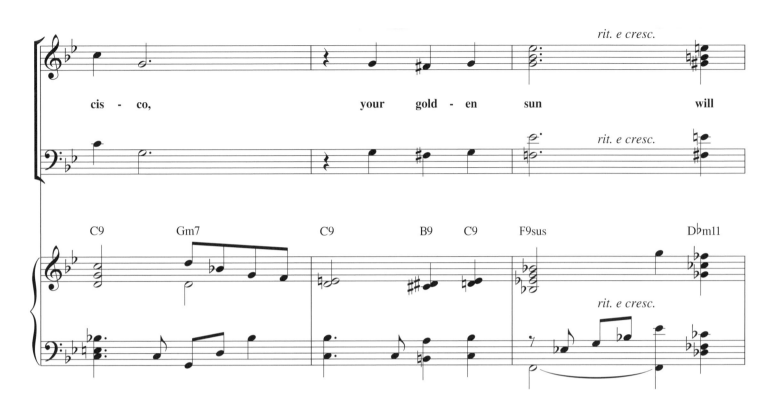

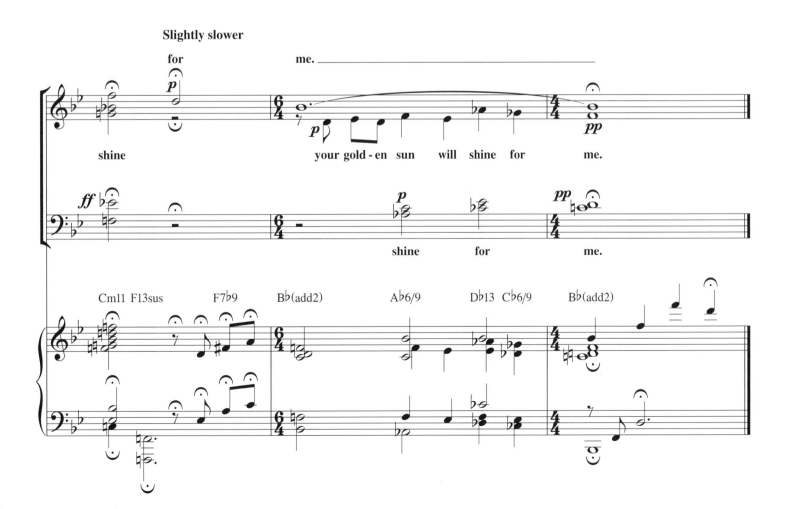

rit. e cresc.
cis - co, your gold - en sun will
rit. e cresc.
C9 Gm7 C9 B9 C9 F9sus D♭m11
rit. e cresc.
Slightly slower
for me.
p
shine your gold - en sun will shine for me.
pp
ff
p
pp
shine for me.
Cm11 F13sus F7♭9 B♭(add2) A♭6/9 D♭13 C♭6/9 B♭(add2)

Kansas City

Words and Music by Jerry Leiber and Mike Stoller
Arranged by Mark Brymer

stand-in' on the cor-ner, Twelfth Street and Vine. __

All **mf**

Stand-in' on the cor-ner, Twelfth Street and Vine. __

Bb6

I'm gon-na be

Stand-in' on the cor-ner, Twelfth Street and Vine, __

stand-in' on the cor-ner,

Eb9

Moon River

from the Paramount Picture BREAKFAST AT TIFFANY'S
Words by Johnny Mercer
Music by Henry Mancini
Arranged by Ed Lojeski

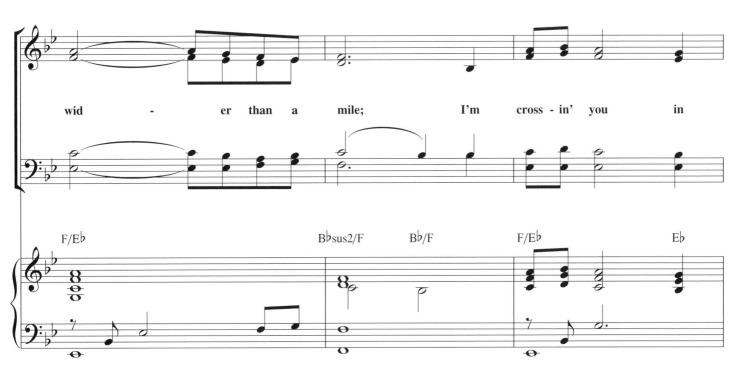

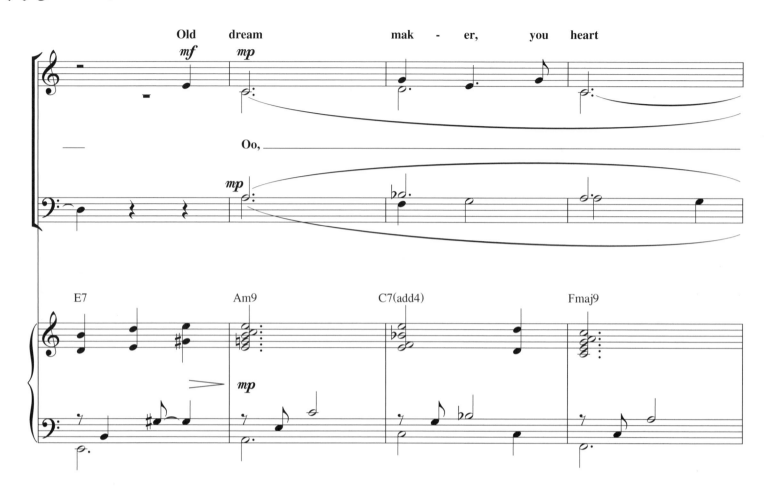

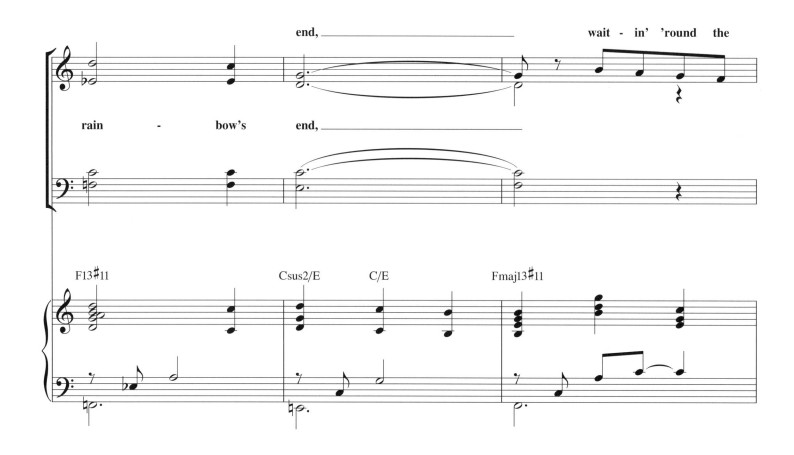

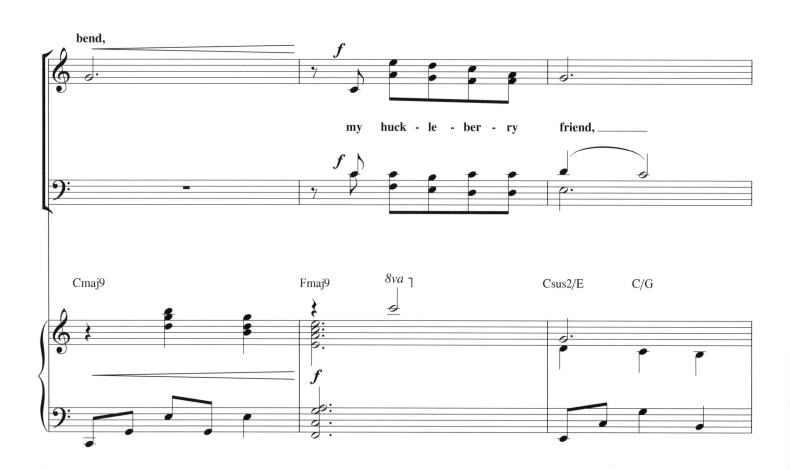

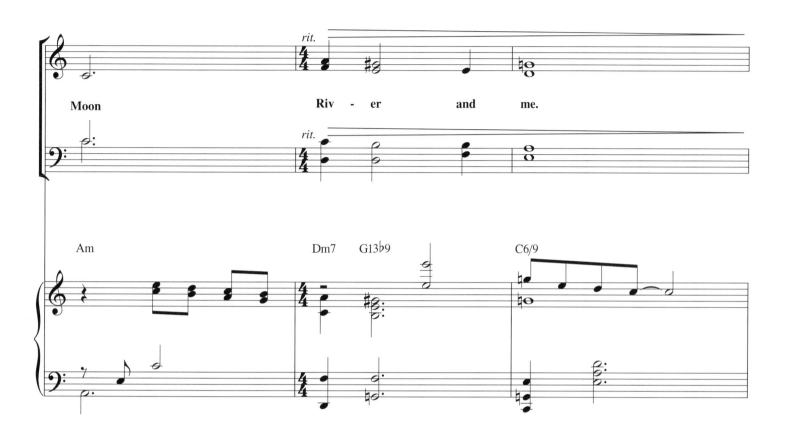

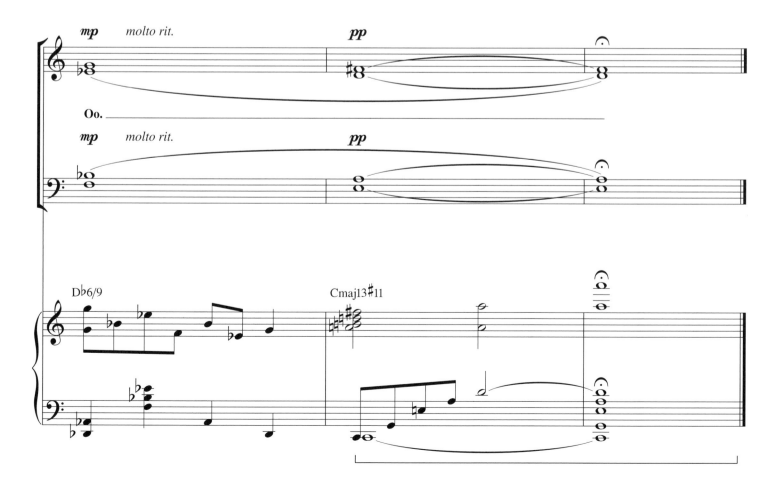

Let It Be

Words and Music by John Lennon and Paul McCartney
Arranged by Kirby Shaw

in my hour __ of dark - ness, ___ she is stand-ing right ___ in front of me, _____

speak-ing words __ of wis - dom, let it be. _____ Let it be, _

__ let it be, __ let it be, _____ let it be. _____

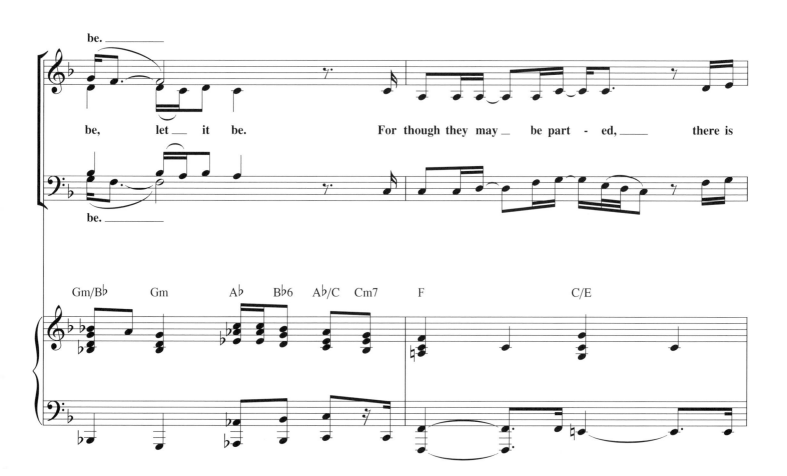

still a chance ___ that they ___ will see, ___ there will be ___ an an - swer, ___ let it

let it

be. ___

be, ___ let it ___ be. ___ Let it be, ___ let it be, ___ let it be, ___

be. ___

There will be ___ an an - swer, ___ there will be ___ an an - swer, ___

F/C   B♭   C   F   B♭/D   C

Suddenly slow

mf Solo
there will be ___ an an - swer, let it   be. _____

Oo. _____

F/A   B♭   C   F/A   B♭   Gm7   C7sus   F

Love Me Tender

Words and Music by Elvis Presley and Vera Matson
Arranged by Roger Emerson

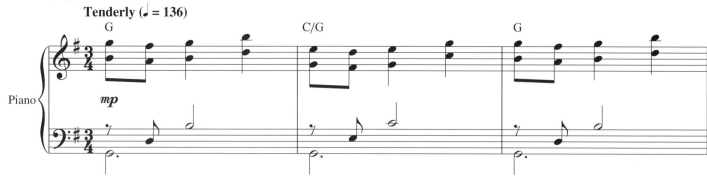

For, my dar - lin', I love you and I al - ways

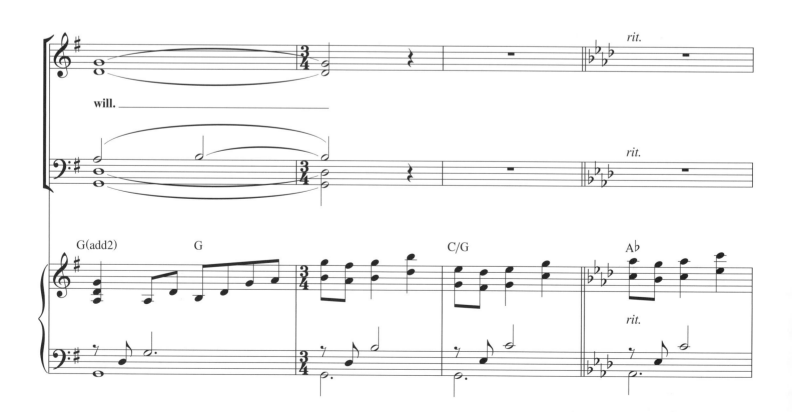

will.

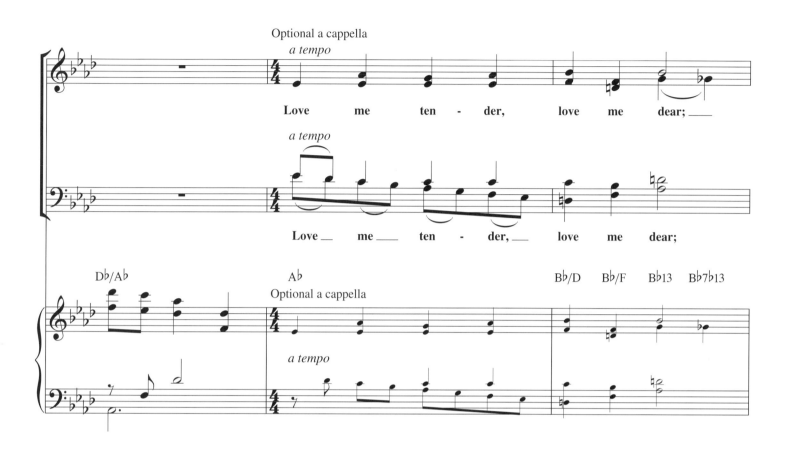

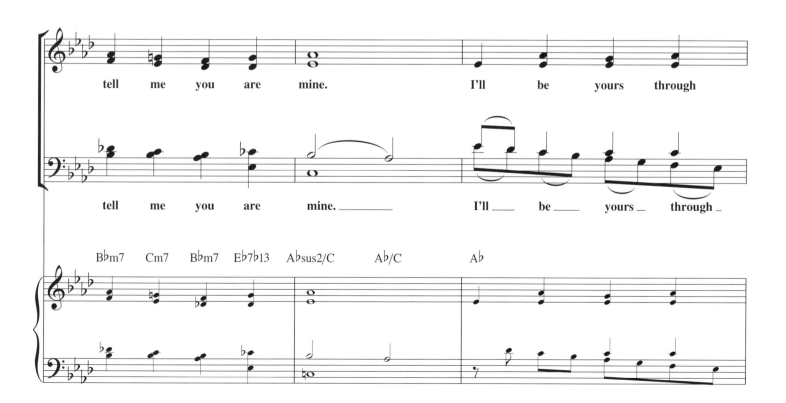

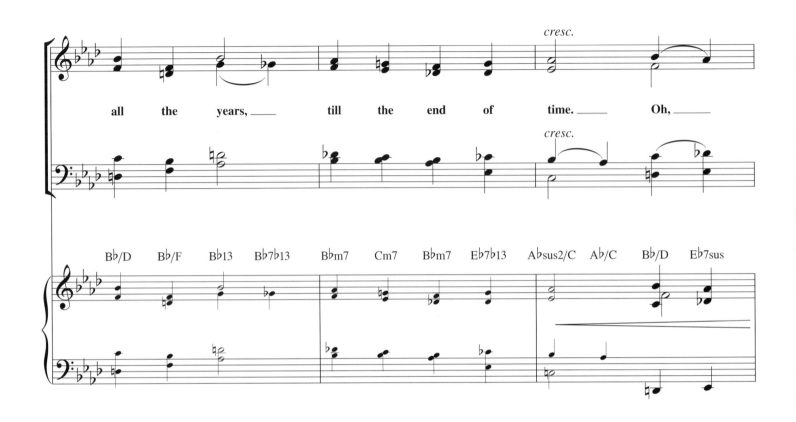

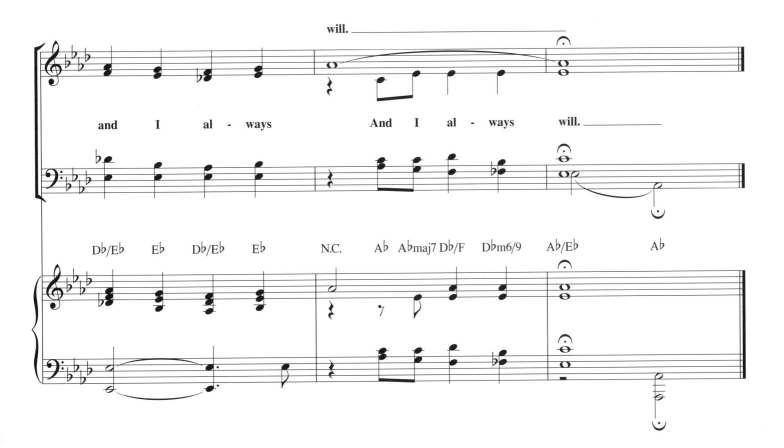

Silver Bells

from the Paramount Picture THE LEMON DROP KID
Words and Music by Jay Livingston and Ray Evans
Arranged by Ed Lojeski

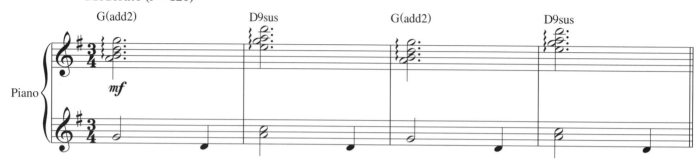

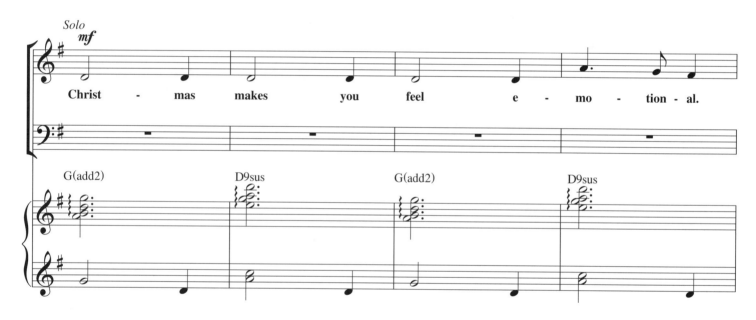

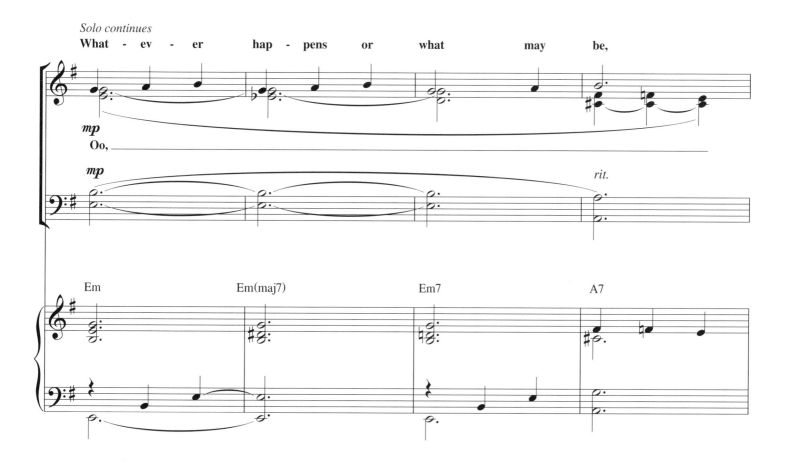

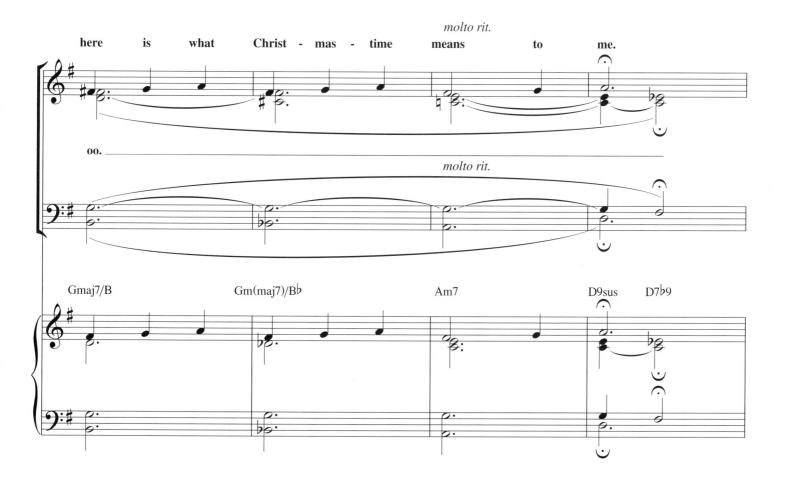

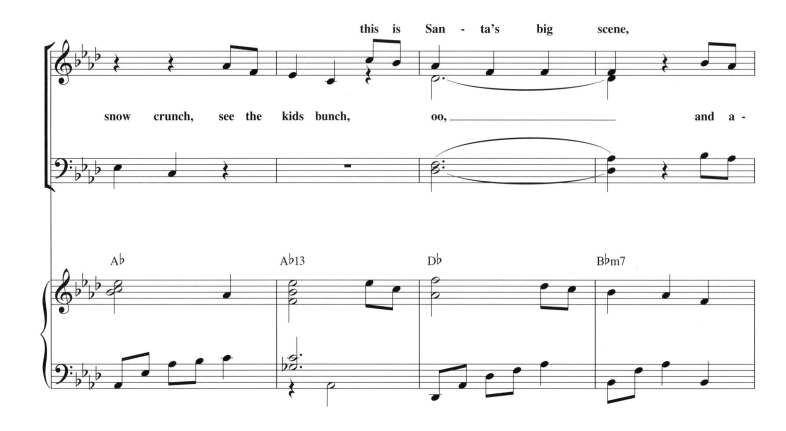

What a Wonderful World

Words and Music by George David Weiss and Bob Thiele
Arranged by Mark Brymer

think _____ to my - self,   what a won - der - ful

world. _____   The

col - ors ___ of the rain - bow, so pret - ty in the sky,

are

al - so ___ on the fac - es of peo - ple go - in' by.

I see

friends shak - in' hands, _____ say - in', "How do you do!"

They're real - ly say - in' "I love you."

I hear

Oo, _____ watch them grow.

ba - bies cry, I watch them grow.

They'll learn much more than I'll _____ ev - er know, and I

think _____ to my - self,   what a won - der - ful

D   A♭m11   D♭7

world. _____   Yes,   I

G♭   D♭m6/F♭   E♭

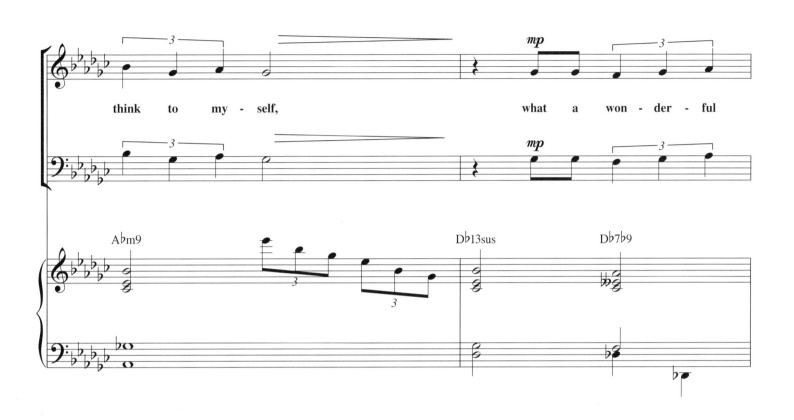

think to my - self, what a won - der - ful

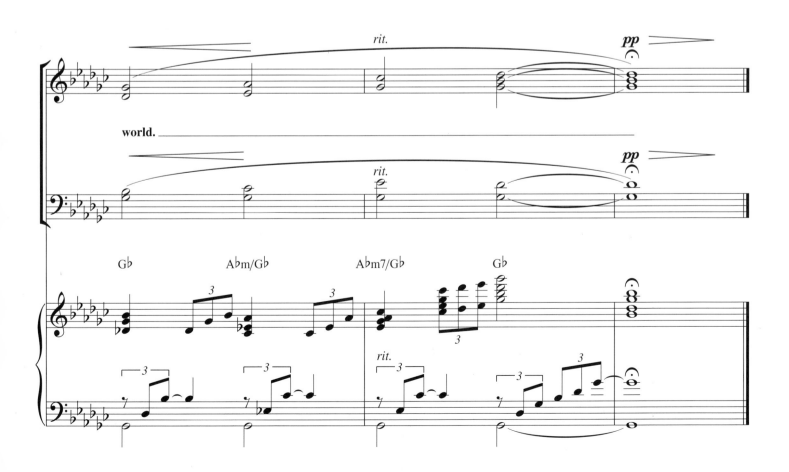

world.

You Are the Sunshine of My Life

Words and Music by Stevie Wonder
Arranged by Mac Huff

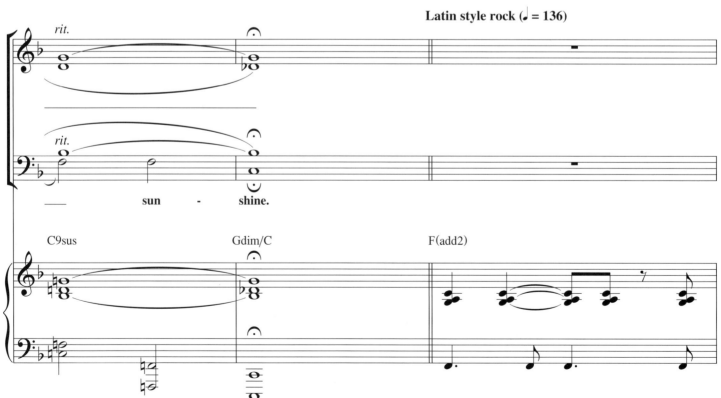

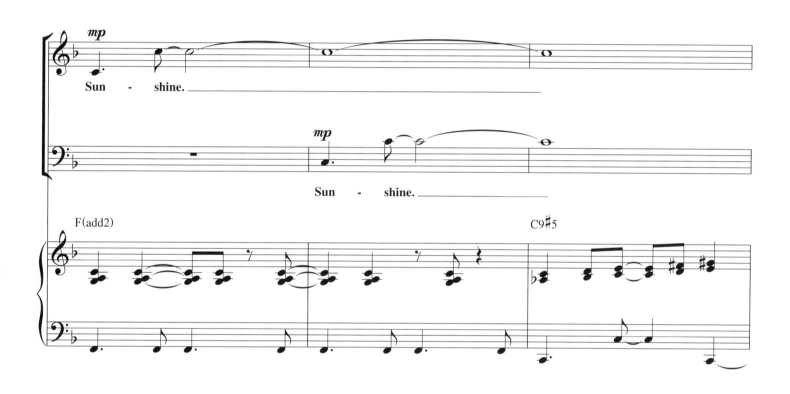

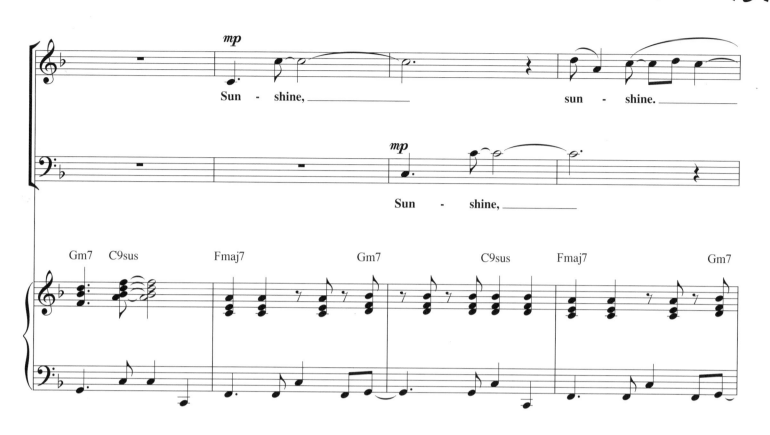

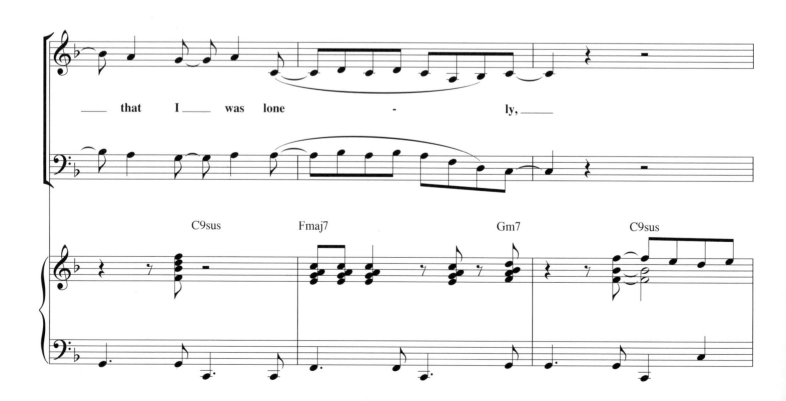

be - cause you   came ____ to   my ____ res - cue; ____

Fmaj9   Gm7   C7sus   A7sus   A7   Am7

____   And   I   know   that ____ this   must ____ be ____

A7   Dmaj7   G   Em7/A

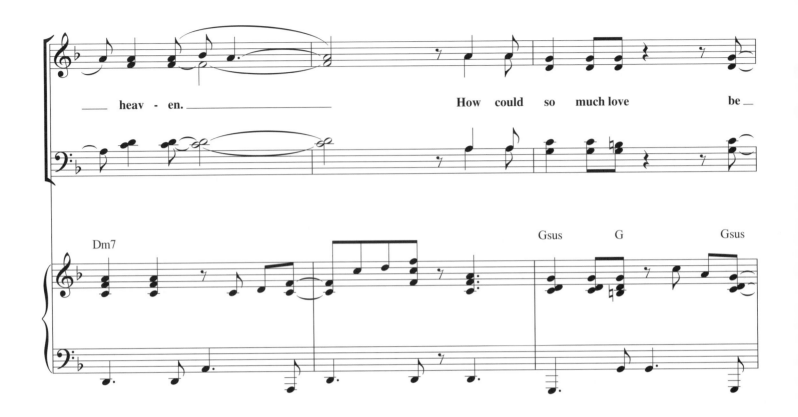

You   are the sun - shine of ____ my life, ____

G6/9   Am11   C6/9   Bm7   Cmaj7   Bm7   B♭7

____   that's why I'll al - ways be ____ a -

Am7   D9sus

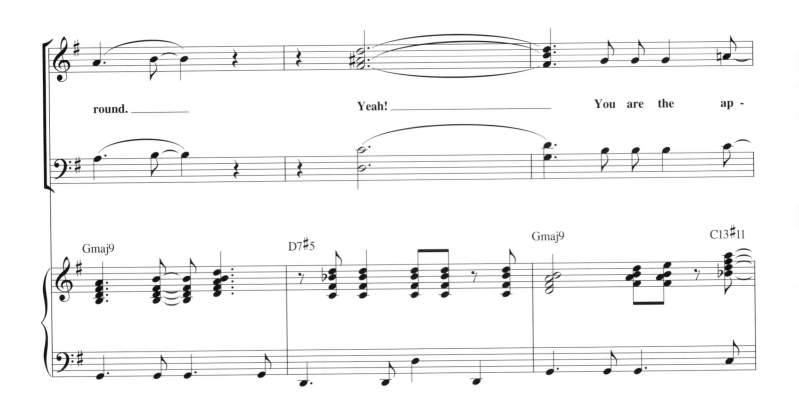

round.   Yeah!   You are the ap -

- ple of   my   eye,

You are the sun - shine _____

Bm7   Em7   Am11   D7♭9

of ___ my life.

Gmaj9

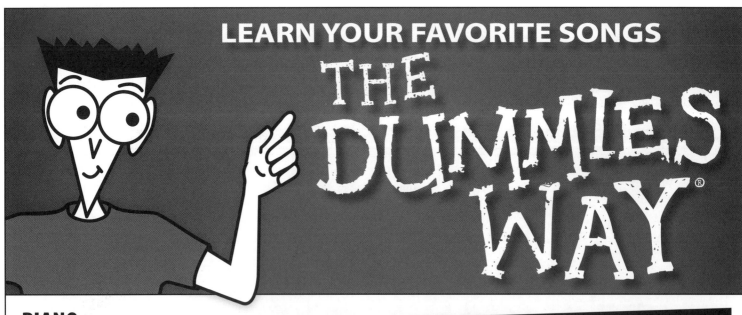